THE HISPANIC INFLUENCE IN THE UNITED STATES

LATINOS
IN AMERICAN HISTORY

GASPAR DE
PORTOLA

BY JIM WHITING

Mitchell Lane
PUBLISHERS

P.O. Box 196
Hockessin, Delaware 19707

THE HISPANIC INFLUENCE IN THE UNITED STATES

LATINOS
IN AMERICAN HISTORY

OTHER TITLES IN THE SERIES

Visit us on the web: www.mitchelllane.com
Comments? email us: mitchelllane@mitchelllane.com

THE HISPANIC INFLUENCE IN THE UNITED STATES

LATINOS
IN AMERICAN HISTORY

GASPAR DE
PORTOLA

BY JIM WHITING

Printing   2   3   4   5   6   7   8   9

Library of Congress Cataloging-in-Publication Data

Whiting, Jim, 1943-
       Gaspar de Portolá/Jim Whiting.
              p. cm. — (Latinos in American history)
       Summary: Describes the life of the seventeenth-century Spanish explorer and first governor of California, Gaspar de Portolá.
       Includes bibliographical references and index
       ISBN 1-58415-148-X (lib bdg.)
       1. Portolâ, Gaspar de—Juvenile literature. 2. Explorers—California—Biography—Juvenile literature. 3. Governors—California—Biography—Juvenile literature. 4. Explorers—Spain—Biography—Juvenile literature. 5. California—History—To 1864—Juvenile literature. [1. Portolâ, Gaspar de. 2. Explorers. 3. Governors. 4. California—History—To 1864.] I. Title. II. Series.
       F864.P8552 W55 2002
       979.4'01'092—dc21
       [B]   2002022143

ABOUT THE AUTHOR: Jim Whiting has been a journalist, writer, editor, and photographer for more than 20 years. In addition to a lengthy stint as publisher of *Northwest Runner* magazine, Mr. Whiting has contributed to the *Seattle Times*, *Conde Nast Traveler*, *Newsday*, and *Saturday Evening Post*. He has edited more than 20 titles in the Mitchell Lane Real-Life Reader Biography series and Unlocking the Secrets of Science. He lives in Washington state with his wife and two teenage sons.

PHOTO CREDITS: Cover: Monterey County Historical Society; p. 6 Hulton/Archive; p. 9 Robert Holmes/Corbis; p. 12 North Wind Picture Archives; p. 14 Hulton/Archive; p. 16, 18 Monterey County Historical Society; p. 22 Catherine Karnow/Corbis; p. 25 Maps.com/Corbis; p. 28 Corbis; p. 32 Bettmann/Corbis; p. 36 Michael T. Sedam/Corbis

PUBLISHER'S NOTE: This story is based on the author's extensive research, which he believes to be accurate. Some parts of the text might have been created by the author based on his research to illustrate what might have happened years ago, and is solely an aid to readability for young adults.

The spelling of the names in this book follow the generally accepted usage of modern day. The spelling of Spanish names in English has evolved over time with no consistency. Many names have been anglicized and no longer use the accent marks or any Spanish grammar. Others have retained the Spanish grammar. Hence, we refer to Hernando de Soto as "de Soto," but Francisco Vásquez de Coronado as "Coronado." There are other variances as well. Some sources might spell Vásquez as Vázquez. For the most part, we have adapted the more widely recognized spellings.

CONTENTS

Hernán Cortes, the discoverer of Baja California. He named it for Queen Califia, a character in a popular book. The Sea of Cortez, which separates Baja California from the mainland of Mexico, bears his name today.

A LAND OF UNDISCOVERED TREASURES

In 1966, a film called *The Russians Are Coming! The Russians Are Coming!* made its debut on movie screens and became very popular. It was a comedy that came out at the height of the Cold War between the Soviet Union (which consisted of Russia and 15 other republics) and the United States. It showed that the two nations could actually work together and become friends.

But almost exactly two centuries earlier, the thought that the Russians were coming was anything but funny to the Spanish authorities who ruled New Spain, which is modern-day Mexico and Central America. They heard reports that Russian fur traders, possibly accompanied by soldiers and settlers, had already crossed the Bering Strait in the North Pacific Ocean to Alaska. That meant that they could be on their way southward along the Pacific Coast toward California, the westernmost of Spain's New World possessions.

Though the Spanish had had a foothold in California for well over two centuries, they had done almost nothing to develop the vast territory during that time. But the fact that the Russians might now be interested suddenly made them very interested themselves.

Spanish interest in the region began in the early 1530s. Hernán Cortés, the conqueror of the Aztec emperor Montezuma and Mexico City in 1521, was looking for new worlds to conquer. He heard rumors of a long island beyond the western coast of Mexico that was inhabited entirely by women warriors known as Amazons.

Written in 1510, a phenomenally successful book called *Las Sergas de Esplandían* by Garcí Rodríguez de Montalvo spoke of an island near the Indies inhabited by such Amazon women. Since at that point no one realized just how wide the Pacific Ocean really was, it seemed possible that this might be the island. According to the book, it was "rich in pearls and gold and peopled with black Amazons whose queen was Calafia."

So Cortés, who had read the book, led an expedition to "Calafia's island" in 1535. In reality, it was a long thin peninsula rather than an island, though it would be more than 170 years before people would realize that fact. Cortés found pearls, but most of them were located in deep water. The tiny colony he established lasted less than a year, and soon Cortés faded from the scene. But the name "California" remained.

In 1542, two Spanish ships under the command of Juan Rodriguez Cabrillo sailed up the west coast as far north as the Oregon border. Cabrillo was searching for the fabled Northwest Passage, which was believed to link the Atlantic and Pacific Oceans. It was a dangerous voyage. The ships had to remain close to shore if the sailors were to spot the elusive passage. But that increased the risk of being blown onto the rocks that lined the shore.

The voyage provided the Spanish with their first glimpse of the westernmost edge of the New World. But it cost Cabrillo his life. He was injured, possibly trying to save his men from an Indian attack, and his wound became infected. He died soon afterward. And he didn't find the Northwest Passage. It doesn't exist.

A few decades later, a profitable trade from the yearly Manila galleon was well under way. Ships loaded with gold and silver taken

This statue of Juan Rodriguez Cabrillo stands in San Diego, California. Cabrillo was the first European to sail up the west coast of California.

from the mines would sail from Acapulco on Mexico's southwestern coast to the Philippine Islands. The gold and silver would be traded in the Philippines for luxury goods, which sold for a huge profit back in Mexico.

The outbound trip to the Philippines took advantage of favorable winds and could be completed in less than three months. But the heavily laden ships took much longer to return after leaving Manila, the main city in the Philippines. Merchants tried to cram as much cargo as they could into the available space, often at the expense of supplies for the crew.

So the long eastward voyage across the Pacific Ocean was hard on the sailors. Spanish authorities thought that perhaps there might be a place along the California coast where the men could land. Then they could stock up on food and fresh water and recover before the final leg to Acapulco.

But there was a problem. When people think of the California coast, they often form a mental picture of long expanses of sandy beaches, with thousands of sunbathers and swimmers in the warm water. That mental picture is correct—for Southern California.

But those beaches are far away from the northern and central California coast where the galleons would normally make their landfall. Much of the coast there is rocky and forbidding, with very few sheltered places where a sailing ship could anchor in safety.

In 1595, a galleon captain named Sebastían Cermeño tried to find a suitable landing spot. He anchored along the coast not far from present-day San Francisco, and noticed white cliffs to the north and seven rocky islands lying to the south that he called the Farallones.

But the spot that Cermeño found was too exposed to be of value. On the orders of the Count of Monte Rey, then the viceroy, or ruler, of New Spain, a ship commanded by Sebastián Vizcaíno (viz-ky-EE-no) set out in 1602 to find a harbor that would be more suitable. He followed Cabrillo's route up the coast and renamed most of the places that Cabrillo had discovered—names that are still in common use.

But after several months at sea, he was in trouble. Most of his men were sick with scurvy, a common disease among sailors on long voyages. Though no one knew it at the time, scurvy is caused by a lack of Vitamin C, which is found in fresh fruits and vegetables. It would weaken men to the point where they could no longer even stand, and it was not unusual for the disease to be fatal.

Vizcaíno knew that he was running out of time. Soon he wouldn't have enough healthy men to work the ship. So when he found an open bay several hundred miles up the coast, he put the best face on his discovery. He said that it was "sheltered from all winds," when in fact it barely qualified as a harbor. He named it Monterey Bay after his sponsor and returned, bearing news of his discovery.

But the Spanish quickly lost interest in what Vizcaíno had located. For one thing, when the galleons sighted California, the hardest part of the trip was over. The winds were generally out of the north and pushed the ships quickly to Acapulco. The impatient crews didn't want to spend any extra time on shore when they were so close to home.

Besides, the land appeared to be desolate and forbidding. As far as the sailors could tell, there didn't seem to be anything worthwhile in this wild new frontier. From the time of their arrival in the New World, the Spanish were obsessed with finding gold. At the same time that Cabrillo was looking for the non-existent Northwest Passage, two lengthy Spanish expeditions were seeking gold. Hernando de Soto was scouring the southern U.S., while Francisco Vásquez de Coronado was riding through the Southwest and Great Plains in searches that became increasingly desperate. Gold simply didn't exist in either location.

But as the California Gold Rush that began in 1848 would demonstrate, there was plenty of gold in California—much of it within 100 miles of Cabrillo's and Vizcaíno's ships. Since the men rarely ventured more than a mile or two inland on the rare occasions when they did come ashore, they had no clue that it was even there.

So Vizcaino's discovery of Monterey became veiled in a fog as thick as the real ones that sometimes blanket the area. The primitive maps of the time still showed that this new land was an island, with the mythical Northwest Passage at its northern end.

A brave Jesuit missionary and explorer proved otherwise. Father Eusebio Francisco Kino founded a mission in northern Sonora, Mexico in 1787. He soon branched out to found many more missions. As Kino moved further west and down into the peninsula that Cortés had tried to settle more than 150 years earlier, he realized that California was not an island at all. He drew up a map that people relied on for many years.

From that point on, what Cortés had hoped was the island of the Amazons was referred to as Baja (lower) California. Everything lying to the north became known as Alta (upper) California.

Not that it made much difference. Without evidence of gold or other riches, there was little reason to explore the area. About 400 people—missionaries, a few soldiers guarding them and their families—were the only Spanish living in California. And they were all in Baja California.

Then a few Russian fur traders changed everything. And an obscure Spanish soldier named Gaspar de Portolá (gahs-PAR-day-port-oh-LA) would carve a place for himself as one of the most important figures in the history of California.■

Jesuit missionaries in California. The Jesuits founded many missions in northern Mexico and Baja California during the late 1600s and 1700s. But their increasing power and wealth alarmed Spain's King Charles III, who eventually ordered them expelled from the New World.

EXPLORING THE FRONTIER

Gaspar de Portolá y de Rovira was born in Balaguer in the Spanish province of Catalonia in 1714. He was the second son of Francisco de Portolá, a member of the noble family of the Barons of Castellnou de Montsec that could trace their ancestry back nearly 500 years. Because his elder brother would inherit the family lands and titles, Gaspar chose a military career and went into the service of the Crown. He would spend the rest of his life as a soldier.

When he was 14, he joined the Regiment of Villaviciosa as a cadet. He slowly moved up the ranks to commissioned ensign, lieutenant and captain and fought with the Spanish army during its campaigns in Italy and Portugal.

In 1764, he was one of a large group of Spanish officers who arrived in New Spain under the command of Lt. General Villalba. Three years later, he was appointed governor of Baja California. He quickly received his first assignment.

Father Kino and his successors had been very successful with their string of missions. Eventually, charges that they were planning on setting up a separate republic were laid against them. While these charges were almost certainly false, Spanish King Charles III was concerned enough about the growing power of the Jesuits to strip

King Charles III of Spain. Soon after expelling the Jesuits from the New World, he learned that the Russians might be on their way to California. So he ordered an expedition to establish settlements and missions there.

them of their leadership and expel them from New Spain. He assigned responsibility for administering the existing missions to two religious orders that could be more easily controlled: the Dominicans and the Franciscans. When the Jesuits were gone, the two orders took over their land, their missions, and their money.

Portolá was placed in command of this effort. Supervising the removal of the Jesuits was an undesirable task, but he exercised much tact and diplomacy in carrying it out. Father Johann Jakob Baegert, a German Jesuit missionary who administered to Indians in Baja California from 1751 to 1768, returned to Germany after being expelled from the region. There he wrote that "Gratitude as well as respect for his good name compels me to state here that Governor Don Gaspar de Portolá treated the Jesuits, considering the circumstances, with respect, honor, politeness, and friendliness. He never caused the least annoyance, sincerely assuring us how painful it was to him to have to execute such a commission. On several occasions tears came to his eyes, and he was surprised to find Europeans willing to live and die in such a country."

But expelling defenseless missionaries must have seemed pretty tame for an experienced veteran of European battlefields. His appointment as governor, though considered a promotion, left him restless because he liked being physically active. He preferred a lifestyle of adventure and discovery over writing reports and being involved in legislation.

Roaming Russians solved the problem.

No sooner had Charles III dealt with the Jesuits than he began receiving reports that Russian fur traders—to be followed perhaps by Russian colonists—might be on their way to the coastal areas that Cabrillo and Vizcaíno had explored and claimed in the name of the Spanish monarchy. Something had to be done—and done quickly.

The Spanish had to occupy Alta California.

In Mexico, Spanish colonial administrator José de Gálvez acted on the king's order. Gálvez began organizing an expedition to set up bases on the California coast in San Diego and Monterey. It would include soldiers, sailors, and Franciscan missionaries. Besides protecting the land from foreign nations, the proposed occupation would give the Spanish opportunities to convert the native peoples to Christianity.

This plan was similar to what had worked well for the Spanish for decades. As they moved forward to a new location, the missionaries would convert many of the natives to Christianity and establish a small town with cultivated fields, orchards and even herds of cattle. The soldiers would provide protection. As each new settlement began to prosper, Spain's power would be slightly increased.

Gálvez gave the name of "The Sacred Expedition" to what was about to begin.

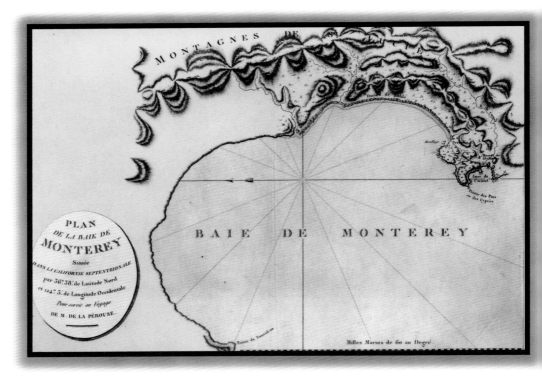

An early map of Monterey Bay. This view is rotated more than 90 degrees to the left. The small point at the bottom of the map is actually at the northern end of the bay.

And Portolá volunteered to lead it.

Portolá's ally among the Franciscans was a remarkable man named Father Junípero Serra. Born in 1713 on the Spanish island of Majorca, he arrived in the New World in 1749 and immediately distinguished himself by walking the nearly 300-mile distance from the port city of Vera Cruz to Mexico City. What was especially remarkable was that he was bitten early in the journey on one of his legs by an insect or spider, which caused swelling and pain that would plague him for the rest of his life. Despite this handicap, he always pushed himself to the limit.

According to the plan laid out by Gálvez, the expedition would originate in Baja California early in 1769 and follow in Cabrillo's and Vizcaíno's long-vanished footsteps. Part of the men would proceed by sea in three ships, with the remainder going overland. All would depart separately but meet in San Diego, which both Cabrillo and Vizcaíno had explored. Their maps demonstrated that it was an excellent harbor. There they would establish a presidio, or army post, and mission. San Diego, it was hoped, would become the first of a string of missions in Alta California similar to those that the Jesuits had established in Baja California.

But the main goal was Monterey and, according to Vizcaíno's enthusiastic report, its excellent harbor. A settlement there would extend the boundary of Spanish power another 400 miles to the north. It would become the new capital of Alta California.

Altogether, less than 300 men would be involved in the attempt to secure Spain's western frontier.

And many of them would be dead before the year was out.■

The Portolá expedition sets off. The men drove several hundred head of cattle to provide food, milk and hides in the new settlements that they planned to establish.

JOURNEY TO SAN DIEGO BAY

The Sacred Expedition began on January 9, 1769 when the first of the three ships, the *San Carlos*, set sail from La Paz, the chief port of Baja California. Gálvez was so eager for the ship to leave that he personally carried some of the mission furniture on board. Besides her crew of over 20 men, she carried Lieutenant Pedro Fages and 25 volunteer soldiers from Portolá's home province of Catalonia. Below decks was a cargo of church ornaments, tools, provisions, and other supplies. The *San Antonio* followed five weeks later, carrying even more cargo. The *San José* was scheduled to depart in June, bearing additional supplies, most of them intended for the force that would make the trip to Monterey.

On March 24, 1769, Captain Fernando de Rivera and Father Juan Crespí led the first land expedition out of Velicatá, the northernmost Spanish outpost in Baja California. Rivera commanded about two dozen cuirassiers, mounted men who wore heavy leather vests that were virtually arrow-proof except at point-blank range. They also carried small shields made from raw bulls' hide to deflect arrows and spears. For even more protection, they wore a type of leather apron that was fastened to the pommel of their saddles. It hung down in front of their legs on both sides. They had three weapons: long lances, broadswords and short muskets. Not surprisingly, they were regarded as excellent warriors.

They were to blaze the trail from Velicatá to San Diego, a distance of about 400 miles. The men encountered constant hardships as they marched through country that was entirely unexplored, crossing deserts, mountains and dry gullies. Despite the difficulties, they arrived in San Diego on May 14.

Portolá led the rest of the land party—about a dozen soldiers and Sergeant José Francisco de Ortega, who would prove to be one of the expedition's most valuable men—and the remaining friars including Father Serra out of Velicatá on May 15. Both his group and Rivera's included Christianized Indians, to demonstrate the advantages of becoming Christians to the Indians they would meet along the way.

Serra's leg quickly became a problem. Portolá tried to convince Serra to rest and let someone else go in his place. Besides the concern for his health, Portolá was afraid the expedition would be delayed if Serra couldn't keep up with them. But Serra was dedicated to founding his missions to introduce the Christian religion to a land of what he considered to be pagans. He refused to surrender to his bad health.

He approached one of the muleteers and asked the man to treat his leg in the same way that he would deal with a sick animal. The muleteer provided a poultice of herbs and mud, and this primitive form of veterinary medicine was enormously successful. Serra was able to continue with his pain much reduced.

As the Portolá expedition continued to march north, the harsh dry terrain gradually grew more green and beautiful. Around June 20th, as the party stood on a hill, much to their joy they saw the gleaming blue waters of the Pacific Ocean. This was a wonderful relief from all the deserts and rough hills they had crossed on their trek. That night they camped by the sea about 80 miles south of San Diego in what is now Ensenada.

When the party reached Rosarito on June 27, they were greeted by an Indian who informed them that San Diego was less than two days ahead. The next morning they were awakened by the sound of pounding hooves. Scouts who had ridden ahead of the party had told Captain Rivera that the Portolá party was on its way. He sent fresh horses to make their final miles easier.

Though some of the Christianized Indians had died during the journey and others deserted, all the Spaniards survived.

But it was a very different story on the two ships. The *San Antonio* had arrived in San Diego after 54 days at sea. But the *San Carlos* met with adverse winds and storms, and its voyage to San Diego lasted twice as long. Scurvy had broken out. Some men had died and the rest were so weakened that they could barely handle the ship.

On June 29, 1769, when Portolá and Serra arrived at San Diego, they were faced with a grim spectacle. Sick men lay in tents and on board the two ships, which were anchored in the bay. The newborn settlement had acquired its first landmark: Puenta de los Muertos, or "Dead Man's Point." More than 20 bodies were already buried there. Over the next few months, they would have lots of company.

The situation was heartbreaking, and at first Portolá did not know what to do. The original plan was for the expedition to proceed north both by sea and by land. With most of the sailors dead or too ill to be effective, that was no longer possible.

But he was still the governor and commander. As a good soldier he knew he had to proceed with his royal instructions to advance to Monterey, even if he didn't have the comforting presence of a ship a few miles offshore. So he courageously marshaled his forces. Time was not on his side. If he waited too long to start, winter snows might block passage across the mountains that he was likely to encounter as he made his way north.

If he was discouraged by the misfortunes, Portolá never wrote about it.

He organized an expedition consisting of Fages and his surviving Catalonians, Rivera and most of the men who had come up from Baja California with him, and Father Crespí. A few muleteers and some of the Indians who had come with them from Baja California also came along. All told, there were about 60 men to face a journey into unknown lands.

Father Serra remained behind with two other friars, the doctor and dozens of sick men. A few soldiers were assigned to guard them.

Neither group felt certain that they would see the other one again.

Portolá and his men had to cross the Santa Lucia Mountains, shown here. Its rugged terrain, steep slopes and deep valleys slowed down the expedition's progress.

THE SEARCH FOR MONTEREY

On the morning of July 14, 1769, the men went to mass. Then Portolá led the way out of the tiny settlement, slightly more than two weeks after his arrival. He left word that when the *San José* arrived, the ship should be directed north to meet him at Monterey. He also held out a very faint hope that enough sailors would recover to take the *San Carlos* back to sea.

He had already scraped together a tiny crew of relatively healthy sailors to man the *San Antonio*. She was slowly making her way back to Mexico with the news of what had happened so far. Then she would return to San Diego with replacement supplies and more men. But Portolá knew that that could take many months.

"I gathered the small portion of food which had not been spoiled in the ships and went on by land to Monterey with that small company of persons, or rather say skeletons, who had been spared by scurvy, hunger, and thirst," he wrote years later.

Because of the weakened condition of the men, progress was slow. The expedition pitched camp early each afternoon so that the scouting force, under the command of Sergeant Ortega, could ride ahead and plan the next day's march. As a result, they would cover between five and 12 miles a day, with complete rests every fourth or fifth day. Their progress was slowed even more because their animals would sometimes stampede. One stampede was caused on July 28 by what would become a regular feature of California living: a series of earthquakes. It was in the vicinity of modern-day Santa Ana.

August 2 was the festival date of Our Lady of the Queen of the Angels, one of the many titles that the church gave to the Virgin Mary. So when the expedition halted and made camp, Crespí gave the name of Nuestra Señora de Los Angeles de Porciúncula to the site. A settlement would eventually be built there. With the name shortened to Los Angeles, it would become one of the largest and most important cities in the world.

While their route had been somewhat inland along relatively easy terrain for the first month, by mid-August they had crossed to the coastline. They proceeded next to the water for several days along the Santa Barbara Channel. The going remained easy. The Indian inhabitants were mainly friendly, and many offered food to the travelers. But even if the natives had wanted to attack Portolá and his men, the fearsome appearance of the cuirassiers would have discouraged them.

Portolá described one of those days, which were among the most pleasant of the entire expedition. "The 18th of August," he wrote, "we proceeded for five hours along the seashore. We halted in a town which had forty or more houses inhabited by over five hundred natives; they made us a present of many fish and we made them a suitable return."

It wasn't until early September, just north of modern-day San Luis Obispo, that the expedition finally encountered enemies who weren't frightened by the heavy weapons the men carried. These were huge grizzly bears. One of them nearly killed a soldier despite being shot nine times. Others attacked the mules before being driven off.

Soon after the battle with the bears, the easy progress was abruptly halted. They reached a point where the Santa Lucia Mountains plunged directly into the sea. That meant that the expedition had to go inland, up into the mountains. But they couldn't go too far away from the coast—they couldn't afford to miss Monterey, especially with the possibility that the Russians might already be there.

As they reluctantly began climbing, they quickly discovered that the going was much slower because of the rugged terrain. They often

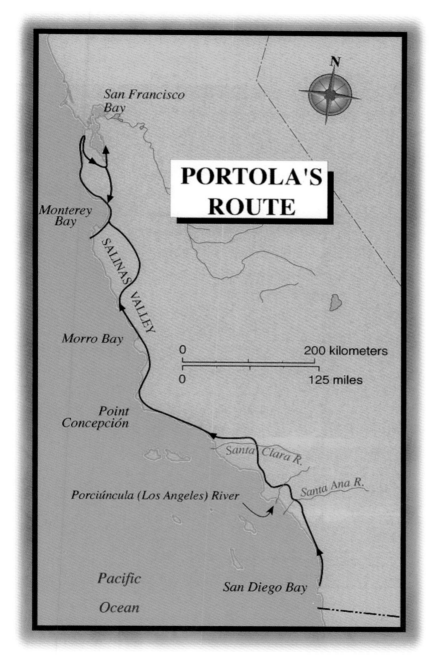

PORTOLA'S ROUTE

San Francisco Bay

Monterey Bay

SALINAS VALLEY

Morro Bay

| 0 | 200 kilometers |
| 0 | 125 miles |

Point Concepción

Santa Clara R.

Santa Ana R.

Porciúncula (Los Angeles) River

Pacific Ocean

San Diego Bay

This map illustrates the route Portola and his men took in 1769 in the search for Monterey Bay.

had to clear paths through brambles and other obstacles. There were additional difficulties. Food was beginning to run low. The weather became much colder. And the dreaded scurvy was on the rise. The men who suffered the worst had to be lashed to uncomfortable wooden frames carried by the mules.

Finally, on September 26, they came down out of the mountains and reached the Salinas River. They followed the river downstream and after marching easily for four days, they could hear the sea beyond some low hills. Scouts sent ahead returned with the reassuring news that no Russians were in sight.

So at dawn on October 1, Portolá and several men climbed to the top of a small hill that overlooked the coast. They spread out Vizcaíno's chart. They saw a point far to the north that corresponded with the chart. Just to their south, there was another point, thickly covered with pine trees. It appeared similar to what Vizcaíno had called the Punta de Pinos, or Point of Pines.

But in between there was only solid coastline, with monotonous sand dunes behind it. The men couldn't see anything even remotely like the famous harbor, which Vizcaíno had described as being "sheltered from all winds."

They spent three more days searching, believing that perhaps they had passed it as they labored through the mountains. Then Portolá called a council of officers to decide what to do. Winter was growing ever closer, food was running short, and more than a dozen men were so ill that they couldn't even move.

There was one other consideration. Using the primitive navigational equipment of his day, Vizcaíno had recorded that Monterey lay at 37 degrees north latitude. Portolá's calculations revealed that they hadn't traveled quite that far.

So after listening to the opinions of the other officers, Portolá made his decision. They would continue north. It was their duty.

With God's aid, they said, we will find it, or perish trying.

Soon virtually every man including Portolá himself was ill, but even from a litter he urged the men forward. They had no more meat or vegetables, so each man existed on bare subsistence rations of five tortillas per day. Three men who were especially close to death were given last rites. Heavy rain soaked them. And still they staggered on.

One thing that helped them to keep going was the rain. For some reason, it reduced and sometimes completely eliminated the symptoms of scurvy, especially the swollen arms and legs that prevented the more seriously ill men from walking. Even the three men who were on the verge of death recovered.

On October 31, the weary explorers staggered to the top of a ridge. The weather had cleared and the sun sparkled off the ocean. They could see an immense bay off in the distance. But nothing about it resembled Monterey.

However, there were prominent white cliffs lying to the north. And far out to sea, they could see seven small rocky islands. These were the Farallones. So the bay did resemble something else: the bay where Cermeño had anchored in 1595.

The situation was obvious. They were too far north.

Somehow, they had missed Monterey.■

This photograph shows an aerial view of San Francisco Bay. It blocked Portolá from going any further north. He didn't realize how important it would become. Today it is one of the two largest ports on the West Coast.

A DISMAL RETURN

Discouraged, the men settled around a campfire and sent Ortega and a few others ahead to try to shoot some deer they saw silhouetted on a hill just to the north. Ortega returned with startling news. He had shot some deer. But standing on top of the hill, he had seen a vast estuary, or arm of the sea. It stretched as far as the eye can see, he told Portolá. It was San Francisco Bay, and they were the first Europeans to sight it. Father Crespí wrote that it was large enough to hold all the ships of Europe.

But what would one day became a flourishing harbor wasn't their objective. Several days of exploration proved that it blocked any further advance to the north.

By now, Portolá was exhausted. He was so upset about not finding Monterey that he didn't realize how important his discovery was. San Francisco Bay would eventually play a far larger role in California's development as one of the West Coast's two largest seaports than Monterey. But Portolá saw the experience as just one more thing to get in the way of his search for Monterey.

He called another council of his officers. They all decided to return to the Point of Pines. From there, a small group of men under Rivera's command headed south. Perhaps Monterey was tucked away in a cleft of the Santa Lucia Mountains. The rest of the men rested and waited.

A week later, Rivera and his men returned, exhausted. Their news was bad. Monterey wasn't there either.

It must have been frustrating for the explorers. There was no harbor sheltered from all winds. A place Vizcaíno had termed "thickly settled with people" was among the most deserted stretches of the entire expedition. In place of the fertile soil that Vizcaíno claimed was suitable for growing crops, there was only sand.

Things were getting truly desperate. Unknown to anyone, the *San José*, which would have provided them with provisions, was lying on the bottom of the ocean hundreds of miles away. The unfortunate ship had sailed as scheduled, returned to port after breaking her foremast, then vanished without a trace following repairs. The *San Carlos* was still anchored in San Diego harbor. Snow was beginning to fall in the nearby mountains. So Portolá called yet another council.

They concluded that there was only one thing to do: return immediately to where they had begun nearly five months earlier. Portolá wrote, "In this confusion and distress, friend, not under compulsion from the Russians, but from keen hunger which was wearing us out, we decided to return to San Diego." While they began to prepare for the long journey back, they grumbled that the Bay of Monterey must have been filled with sand for them to have missed it.

So they put up a prominent cross that would be clearly visible from several miles out at sea. Underneath it they buried a bottle that contained a description of what had happened during the entire expedition. Then they departed on December 10.

They retraced their steps back up the Salinas River, then began the hardest part of the trip. They had to re-cross the Santa Lucia Mountains. But with the aid of many geese that they shot and killed that eased their hunger pangs, the expedition took just over a week to retrace their path through the rugged peaks. On January 3, they passed Point Concepción, where the coastline makes an abrupt turn and runs nearly east and west.

This area along the Santa Barbara Channel had been the scene of their most pleasant journeying on the way north, and the return proved to be the same. The warm sun helped the men who were still sick to recover. The trail was flat and easy to follow. And best of all, the starving men began finding abundant food, much of it donated by the generous Indians. The worst was over, and three weeks later they entered San Diego. They were starved, exhausted, and depressed, but they were grateful to have returned to the colony safely.

Portolá wrote, "On this day we arrived at San Diego, giving thanks to God that, notwithstanding the great labors and privations we had undergone, not a single man had perished. Indeed we had accomplished our return march, through the great providence of God, without other human aid except that, when we were in dire need, we killed some mules for our necessary substance."

In one sense, what Portolá had done was extraordinary. He had led a small, ill-equipped expedition for more than half a year over nearly 1,000 miles of virtually uncharted wilderness. The men had been confronted by cold, rain, disease, near-starvation and many other hardships. Yet not a single man under Portolá's command had died.

But in another, more important sense, he had failed.

He hadn't found Monterey.■

Father Junípero Serra. Despite some physical ailments, he drove himself tirelessly to spread the Christian faith to the Indians in California. He began what would become a string of 19 missions from San Diego to north of San Francisco. Many people consider him the "Father of California."

ONE MORE CHANCE

CHAPTER 6

As Portolá's weary men marched back into the tiny settlement, there was a joyful reunion with the men who had remained behind. Portolá found that the three Franciscan fathers had managed to survive, even though nearly 20 more men had died of scurvy. Even Father Serra himself had been briefly ill with the disease.

Beside scurvy, the Spaniards at San Diego had other worries. Relations with some of the Indians who lived near the settlement had become strained, and there had been one pitched battle. One young soldier was killed by an arrow through his throat, and one of the friars was wounded in the hand. But several Indians had been shot, and fear of Spanish muskets was enough to keep them from launching further attacks.

And the *San Antonio* still had not returned from Mexico with additional supplies, so the entire colony was threatened with starvation. The shortage of food was made even more critical when Portolá and his men returned, because this meant many more mouths to feed.

Portolá carefully calculated how much longer their existing food would last. Then he set a date of March 20. If the relief ship didn't appear by then, the entire expedition would have to return to its starting point without discovering Monterey. They would also have to abandon even the tiny settlement at San Diego.

Serra was bitterly disappointed. He wrote, "There is even talk of abandonment and suppression of my poor little mission in San Diego. May God avert such a tragedy."

As the dreaded day when they would be forced to depart grew closer, Serra, Crespí and the other Franciscans began a novena, or nine-day devotion, in honor of St. Joseph, the patron saint of the expedition. It would end with a feast on the day before Portolá's deadline.

Father Crespí wrote that "On the very day of the feast, March 19th, on which a high mass had been sung, a sermon preached, and at which many confessions were heard, and communions received, at about three o'clock in the afternoon, we saw outside of our desired port a ship that was coming supplied with every kind of provision."

The ship, which had been sighted far out at sea, continued on past the anxious watchers. But Portolá decided to delay the scheduled departure. Five days later the ship returned and entered the harbor. It was the *San Antonio*, and she saved the expedition.

From then on, Father Serra celebrated a high mass on the 19th of every month for the saving of San Diego and the first California mission.

In addition to the badly needed supplies, the *San Antonio* also brought a letter from Gálvez, "encouraging" Portolá not to give up. After conferring with his chief officers, Portolá felt that perhaps they had actually reached Monterey but had failed to recognize it.

Father Serra was even more certain.

When Portolá had returned with the news that he hadn't found Monterey, a strained Serra snapped, "You come from Rome without having seen the Pope."

So Portola decided to go back to Punta de Pinos. With plenty of fresh supplies, he was once again able to make plans.

He would lead another land expedition over the route they'd pioneered the previous year. And the *San Antonio* would make her way up the coast with Serra aboard.

The ship departed on April 16, 1770. Portolá rode out the following day. A handful of men remained behind in San Diego to guard the settlement.

With a much smaller group and traveling over now-familiar terrain, Portolá's expedition took just 36 days this time. The previous northward journey had taken nearly double that amount of time.

Arriving at Punta de Pinos, they went to the cross they'd erected more than six months earlier and discovered that some of the local Indians, apparently believing in its magical powers, had put feathers, fish and food around its base. And as they walked along the beach, they looked out over the calm water. Seeing seals and spouting whales, they finally decided that they were in fact at Vizcaíno's Monterey.

A week later, on May 31, the *San Antonio* came in sight. Portolá's men lit three signal fires to let the ship's crew know that they were there. The ship anchored nearby, and Father Serra jubilantly came ashore.

On June 3, in front of an open-air altar, Father Serra conducted a formal mass. In place of music, the soldiers fired their muskets and the *San Antonio* answered with the boom of her cannons. Serra blessed a large cross and sprinkled holy water on the earth around the assembled company.

When the religious rites were completed, Portolá performed a civic ceremony. He unfurled the royal standards and took possession of Monterey—as well as Alta California—in the name of the Spanish King.

The good soldier had done his duty.■

Fort Ross, the scene of a Russian colony in California between 1812 and 1841. It is located near Bodega Bay, north of San Francisco. Today it is a state park.

THE
ACCOMPLISHMENT

After fulfilling his mission, Portolá followed the orders of his superiors and appointed Fages as military commander, with Serra also remaining as president of the missions. Portolá sailed away from Monterey on July 9 and returned to Mexico. He would never see California again.

The news of Portolá's success was greeted enthusiastically in Mexico City. Church bells rang out and the government printed a pamphlet with some of the details of the expedition. Galvéz described its leader in glowing terms: "It is here at this moment in which Portolá is receiving his deserved reward of compliments and congratulations from superiors, companion in arms, and the people of Mexico, that I feel it necessary to underline the fact that in all the documents I have examined, I have scarcely come across one word of self-praise for himself or his deeds, well justified though it would have been, but only praise for the success of the expedition achieved by his men, for the missionaries and for the higher authorities who planned it. All through the march we never find him losing his temper, never failing in his honor or his professional military character, never questioning an order, never giving an order that was not well thought out and worth giving."

Despite this public praise, the rest of Portolá's career was relatively quiet. He was promoted to lieutenant colonel, then to colonel. In 1776 he became governor of Puebla in central Mexico.

He returned to Spain in 1784. The following year, by royal decree, he was granted a post as colonel attached to the Numancia Regiment in Barcelona. He was named royal deputy of the city of Lérida and its castles early in 1786. Later that year, after a short illness, Gaspar de Portolá died. He was buried in the military tombs of the parish of St. Peter in Lérida. To show his love for the province of his birth and to the city of Lérida, Portolá donated all his possessions for use in charitable work.

Perhaps because he left California immediately following the founding of Monterey, Portolá didn't become well-known in the future U.S. state. A logging town south of San Francisco originally known as Searsville eventually changed its name to Portola Valley and became one of California's wealthiest communities. Several California schools were named for him. That was about all.

He began to receive wider recognition in 1969 and 1970 as California celebrated its bicentennial—which was dated from his expedition. Several statues were erected in Catalonian and California cities with which he was connected.

He received further honors in October 1986 on the bicentenary of his death. Prominent people from both Spain and the United States participated in ceremonies that culminated when the Postmaster General of Spain issued a commemorative stamp of Governor Portolá marking a map of California.

Portolá's accomplishments are considered even more remarkable because, according to Joshua Paddison in *A World Transformed*, though Portolá was a seasoned military officer, "He was not an experienced explorer nor particularly comfortable in the wilderness."

After Portolá's departure, Father Serra's energy continued at a high level. The expedition had revealed that there were many more natives than had originally been estimated. That meant an increase in the number of missions, to ensure that the Franciscans could introduce the Christian religion to everyone.

In addition to San Diego and Monterey, he founded seven more missions before his death in 1784. His successors would add 12 more to the total. They were situated about a day's journey from each other, and played an important part in California's development during the next decades. Many became the sites of future cities. So Father Serra came to be regarded as the real founder of California by many people.

Though it encountered some difficult days, Monterey remained the capital of Alta California until 1846, when the Mexican-American war broke out. A group of American sailors soon captured the town, and California was given to the victorious U.S in 1848. By 1850, it had become a state and the first capital was located in San José.

But Monterey remains a popular tourist town. Just to the south, in land that in Portola's time was barren and virtually uninhabited, are the exclusive towns of Carmel and Pacific Beach.

The state's namesake is still remembered too, in Disney's California Adventure theme park which opened in 2001 in Anaheim. One of its attractions is called "Golden Dreams," a theater that features a 22-minute film describing what immigrants to California had to give up to realize their dreams. The film is narrated by "Queen Calafia," whose actual voice is Whoopi Goldberg.

And what about the Russians? Did they ever come?

In 1799, Russian fur traders founded Sitka, Alaska. But within a few years the new settlement began running short of food. Some of the desperate colonists sailed to San Francisco to obtain supplies.

That contact led to an expedition in 1812 that established a Russian colony on the northern California coast above Bodega Bay, about a two-hour drive today from San Francisco. It was called Fort Ross from a shortened form of "Rossiya," a different spelling of Russia.

The new arrivals concentrated on hunting sea otters for several years, but the animals were soon depleted. So the colony switched to agriculture. But that was never successful and in 1841 the Russians departed, as peacefully as they had come. They left very little behind to mark their passing. Apart from the site of the fort itself, about the only other reminder of their 29 years in the U.S. is the nearby Russian River, renamed from the original "Slavyanka." Fort Ross currently exists as a state park, and visitors can wander through buildings that have been reconstructed to resemble the original settlement.

And with the wind off the sea whistling through the tall grass, perhaps they can let their imaginations wander a little.

If Portolá and his tiny expedition had failed in its mission, all of California would have remained open. The Russians might then have been more aggressive. Or the British. Or someone else.

If that had happened, it is possible that California could have been settled and developed by some other country to a much greater degree than the Spanish were able to do. This could have been accomplished long before the new United States was powerful enough to extend its reach that far west. In that case, its expansion might have been halted.

So although it was certainly not their intention, as Captain Gaspar de Portolá, Father Junípero Serra and a small band of men stood near the beach on that June day in 1770, they may have made the last line of the song "America the Beautiful" possible.

That nation—which would be born six years later—would indeed stretch "from sea to shining sea." ■

CHRONOLOGY

1714   Born in Balaguer in the Spanish province of Catalonia

1728   Goes into military service as a cadet

1764   Arrives in New Spain

1767   Appointed governor of Baja California

1768   Volunteers to command "Sacred Expedition" to secure Spain's California claim

1769   Departs for Monterey, but fails to recognize it from description; discovers San Francisco Bay

1770   Returns to San Diego without having found Monterey; organizes another expedition, which finds Monterey and claims it in the name of the king of Spain

1771   Promoted to lieutenant colonel and later to colonel

1776   Becomes governor of Puebla in central Mexico.

1784   Returns to Spain

1785   Is given a post as colonel of regiment in Barcelona

1786   Is named royal deputy of the city of Lérida. Dies on October 10 after a short illness

TIMELINE IN HISTORY

1492	Christopher Columbus discovers the New World
1513	Vasco Núñez de Balboa becomes the first European to gaze on the Pacific Ocean
1535	Hernán Cortés arrives in Baja California to establish a colony for Spain, but departs within a year
1542-43	Expedition of Juan Rodriguez Cabrillo and Bartolomé Ferrelo explores California coast as far north as Oregon border
1579	Francis Drake lands just north of San Francisco Bay and claims land he finds for Queen Elizabeth
1602	Sebastián Vizcaíno sails up California coast and discovers Monterey, but exaggerates his description in his report
1607	Jamestown becomes first permanent English settlement in New World
1697	Jesuits establish Nuestra Señora de Loreto, first of 23 missions in Baja California
1720	Mission at La Paz in Baja California is established
1767	Spanish King Charles III orders the expulsion of all Jesuits in New Spain. Governor Portolá is given the responsibility of supervising the expulsion

1768	Inspector General José de Gálvez organizes land and sea expeditions to occupy Alta California; Portolá volunteers as commander
1769	The *San Carlos*, the *San Antonio*, and later the *San José* set sail for San Diego; two land parties also strike out for San Diego
1770	Portolá establishes settlement at Monterey
1772	Viceroy of Mexico orders Don Pedro Fages to undertake another voyage of exploration to California
1775	Exploration of San Francisco Bay undertaken by Juan de Ayala on the *San Carlos*
1776	Declaration of Independence is signed, freeing 13 North American colonies on the East Coast from Great Britain's rule; Monterey is named capital of Alta and Baja California

FOR FURTHER READING

Denevi, Don, and Noel Francis Moholy. *Junípero Serra: The Illustrated Story of the Franciscan Founder of California's Missions*. New York: Harper & Row, 1985.

Galvin, John (editor). *A Journal of Explorations: Northward along the Coast of Monterey in the Year 1775*. San Francisco: John Howell Books, 1964.

Johnson, Paul C. *Pictorial History of California*. Garden City, NY: Doubleday and Company, 1970.

King, Kenneth M. *Mission to Paradise: The Story of Junípero Serra and the Missions of California*. Chicago: Franciscan Herald Press, 1956, 1975.

Maynard J., O.F.M. (editor). *Life of Fray Junípero Serra*. Washington, DC: Academy of American Franciscan History, 1955.

Paddison, Joshua (editor). *A World Transformed: Firsthand Accounts of California Before the Gold Rush*. Berkeley, CA: Heyday Books, 1999.

Pourade, Richard F. *The History of San Diego: The Explorers*. San Diego: The Union-Tribune Publishing Company, 1960.

Rose, Robert Selden. "The Portolá Expedition of 1769-1770: Diary of Vicente Vila" in Publications of the Academy of Pacific Coast History, Vol. II (1911).

Ruscin, Terry. *Mission Memoirs*. Edited by Sue Diaz. San Diego: Sunbelt Publications, 1999.

Smith, Donald Eugene and Frederick J. Teggert (editors). "Diary of Gaspar de Portolá During the California Expedition of 1769-1770" in Publications of the Academy of Pacific Coast History, Vol. III (1909).

The Spanish West by the editors of Time-Life Books. New York: Time-Life Books, 1976.

Teggert, Frederick J. (Editor). "Diary of Miguel Costansó" in Publications of the Academy of Pacific Coast History, Vol. I (1910).

ON THE WEB

Encyclopedia.com
http://www.encyclopedia.com/html/P/Portola.asp

Portolá's Statue
http://www.ci.pacifica.ca.us/HISTORY/portola.html

The Portolá Expedition of 1769
http://users.dedot.com/mchs/portola1769.html

San Diego Biographies
http://www.sandiegohistory.org/bio/portola/portola.htm

Kino Missions
http://www.nps.gov/tuma/Kino_Missions.html

The Portolá Association
http://www.portola-assoc.org/english/index2.htm

GLOSSARY

alta (ALL-tuh): Spanish word meaning "upper"

baja (BA-ha): Spanish word meaning "lower"

colony (CALL-uh-nee): a group of people who leave their native country to settle a new land; a settlement subject to, or connected with, a parent nation

cuirassier (KWIR-uh-sir): a cavalry soldier wearing defensive armor for the torso comprising of a breastplate and back plate, originally made of leather; Spanish cuirassiers were also known as buffcoats

diplomacy (di-PLO-muh-see): ability to handle talks between two parties without jeopardizing the peace

Dominican (dough-MIN-ih-can): a member of an order of friars founded by St. Dominic in 1215, especially known for their dedication to preaching

expedition (ex-puh-DISH-un): an excursion, journey, or voyage made for a specific purpose such as war or exploration; also, the group of people involved in this activity

Farallones (FAIR-uh-lawns): rocky islands

fortitude (FOR-ti-tood): strength of mind that gives a person courage in the face of danger

Franciscan (fran-SIS-can): a member of the Order of Friars Minor founded by St. Francis of Assisi in 1209; known especially for their dedication to preaching, missionary work, and charities

Jesuit (JES-oo-it): a member of the Society of Jesus founded by St. Ignatius Loyola in 1534; known especially for their dedication to missionary and educational work

league (leeg): a unit of measure that can vary from 2.4 to 4.6 miles

litter (LIT-ur): a bed or stretcher used to carry a sick or injured person

Manila galleon (man-ILL-uh GAL-ee-un): Spanish trading ship that traveled between Mexico and the Philippines

muleteer (MYOOL-teer): a person who drives mules

poultice (POLE-tiss): moist, soft healing substance applied to an inflamed part of the body to provide relief

presidio (preh-SID-ee-oh): headquarters of military authorities

scurvy (SKUR-vee): disease caused by a lack of vitamin C, marked by swollen, bleeding gums and sore red spots on the skin. Often fatal

seismic (SYZ-mik): relating to vibrations in the earth, such as those caused by earthquakes

subsist (sub-SIST): to nourish oneself (with food)

viceroy (VYC-uh-roy): the governor of a country ruled by a king or other sovereign

INDEX